Table Of Contents

Chapter 6: Understanding Ad Campaign Types

- Search Ads: Reaching Users at the Right Moment
- Display Ads: Building Brand Awareness
- Video Ads: Engaging Through Visual Storytelling
- Shopping Ads: Showcasing Products Effectively
- App Promotion Ads: Driving App Installs and Engagement

Chapter 7: Mastering Ad Extensions

- Using Sitelink, Callout, and Structured Snippet Extensions
- Leveraging Location and Affiliate Extensions
- Showcasing Additional Information with Promotion Extensions

Chapter 8: Bidding Strategies and Budgeting

- Manual vs. Automated Bidding Strategies
- Setting Realistic Budgets for Campaigns
- Adjusting Bids for Optimal Performance

Chapter 9: Monitoring and Optimization

- Tracking Conversions and KPIs
- Analyzing Performance Data
- A/B Testing: Optimizing Ads for Better Results

Chapter 10: Advanced Techniques and Tips

- Remarketing: Reconnecting with Interested Users
- Dynamic Search Ads: Targeting Relevant Searches Automatically
- Ad Schedule and Geo-Targeting: Reaching the Right Audience at the Right Time
- Using Negative Keywords to Refine Audience Targeting

Chapter 11: Staying Up-to-Date with Google Ads

- Keeping Abreast of Google Ads Updates

Whether you're a business owner looking to promote your products, a marketer aiming to master online advertising, or an aspiring digital entrepreneur, "Google Ads Blueprint" will equip you with the knowledge and practical skills needed to create, launch, and optimize successful Google Ads campaigns. With a comprehensive blend of strategic insights, step-by-step instructions, and real-world case studies, this book will guide you towards harnessing the power of Google Ads to grow your business and achieve your advertising goals.

Introduction

In the ever-evolving landscape of digital marketing, one platform has consistently stood out as a beacon of opportunity and success: Google Ads.

With its immense reach, precision targeting, and measurable results, Google Ads has revolutionized the way businesses connect with their target audiences and drive growth.

This introductory chapter sets the stage for our journey into the world of Google Ads, where we will explore its power and understand why it has become an essential tool for businesses seeking exponential expansion.

Understanding the Power of Google Ads

Imagine having the ability to present your products or services to potential customers precisely when they're searching for them. This is the power that Google Ads bestows upon businesses. Google, the world's most popular search engine, processes over 3.5 billion searches every day. Each of these searches represents a potential opportunity for your business to be discovered by users actively seeking solutions to their needs. Google Ads allows you to capitalize on this vast user base and display your ads at the very moment users are expressing interest in your offerings.

Through its advanced targeting capabilities, Google Ads enables you to reach the right audience with the right message. Whether it's based on keywords, demographics, interests, or even user behavior, you have the ability to tailor your campaigns to reach those most likely to convert. This level of precision not only enhances your ad's relevance but also maximizes your return on investment (ROI) by ensuring that your budget is spent on users who are genuinely interested in what you have to offer.

Why Google Ads is Essential for Business Growth

In today's digital age, a strong online presence is non-negotiable for businesses that aim to thrive. Traditional advertising methods, while still relevant, often lack the level of specificity and measurability that online advertising provides. This is where Google Ads shines as a beacon of efficiency and effectiveness.

1. **Targeted Reach:** Unlike traditional advertising, where you cast a wide net and hope to catch a few interested leads, Google Ads allows you to target your ideal customers directly. By selecting relevant keywords and demographics, you can ensure that your ads are shown only to those who are most likely to convert.

2. **Immediate Results:** With Google Ads, you don't have to wait for weeks or months to see the impact of your advertising efforts. As soon as your campaigns are live, your ads start appearing on search engine results pages and across the Google Display Network, generating traffic and potential leads from day one.

3. **Measurable ROI:** The ability to track every click, conversion, and interaction with your ads provides invaluable insights into the performance of your campaigns. You can see exactly how your budget is being utilized and make data-driven decisions to optimize your strategy for better results.

4. **Flexibility and Control:** Google Ads offers a high degree of flexibility, allowing you to adjust your campaigns in real-time based on performance data. If a particular keyword is driving significant traffic but not converting, you can refine your strategy to target more relevant keywords instead.

5. **Scalability:** As your business grows, so can your Google Ads campaigns. With the right strategies in place, you can scale your advertising efforts to reach new markets, expand your product offerings, and stay ahead of competitors.

In this book, we will delve deep into the intricacies of Google Ads, exploring how to create compelling ads, select the right keywords, design effective landing pages, and optimize your campaigns for maximum impact. By the end of this journey, you will be equipped with the knowledge and skills to harness the true potential of Google Ads and drive unparalleled business growth in the digital landscape. So, let's embark on this exciting adventure and unlock the secrets to mastering Google Ads!

Chapter 1: Getting Started with Google Ads

In this chapter, we'll lay the foundation for your Google Ads journey. We'll guide you through the process of setting up your account, understanding the platform's structure, and preparing to launch your first successful advertising campaign.

Navigating the Google Ads Platform

The Google Ads platform is your gateway to creating, managing, and optimizing your advertising campaigns. As you embark on your journey, familiarize yourself with the different sections and tools within the platform:

1. **Dashboard:** Your main hub for accessing campaign data, performance metrics, and important notifications.
2. **Campaigns:** This is where you'll create and manage your advertising campaigns, each with its specific goals and settings.
3. **Ad Groups:** Within each campaign, you'll organize your ads and keywords into ad groups, allowing for better targeting and organization.
4. **Keywords:** The foundation of your campaigns, keywords are the terms users search for that trigger your ads.
5. **Ads:** Craft compelling ad copy and visuals to entice users and drive them to your website or landing page.
6. **Extensions:** Enhance your ads with additional information like location, phone number, site links, and more.
7. **Audiences:** Tailor your ads to specific user groups based on demographics, interests, and behaviors.
8. **Settings:** Configure campaign settings such as budget, bidding strategy, and scheduling.

Creating Your Google Ads Account

Before you can dive into creating campaigns, you need to create a Google Ads account. Here's how:

1. **Visit Google Ads:** Go to the Google Ads website and click on the "Get Started" or "Start Now" button.
2. **Sign In or Sign Up:** If you have a Google account, sign in. If not, you'll need to create one.
3. **Choose Your Goal:** Google Ads will prompt you to select a goal for your advertising campaign, such as website visits, sales, or calls.
4. **Campaign Type:** Based on your goal, choose the appropriate campaign type (e.g., Search, Display, Video, etc.).
5. **Campaign Details:** Enter the details of your campaign, including the campaign name, geographic targeting, budget, and bidding strategy.
6. **Ad Group Creation:** Within your campaign, create ad groups. Each ad group should focus on a specific product, service, or category.

Understanding Account Structure: Campaigns, Ad Groups, and Keywords

A well-organized account structure is crucial for effective Google Ads management. Let's break down the hierarchy:

1. **Campaigns:** These are the top-level entities where you set your campaign's objective, budget, and other overarching settings. For example, if you're a bakery, you might have a "Summer Specials" campaign.
2. **Ad Groups:** Within each campaign, you'll have multiple ad groups. Ad groups house a set of related ads and keywords. For your bakery campaign, ad groups could be "Cakes," "Cookies," and "Bread."
3. **Keywords:** Keywords are the terms you choose to trigger your ads. They are linked to specific ad groups. For the "Cakes" ad group, keywords could include "birthday cakes," "wedding cakes," etc.

By maintaining a structured account, you can better manage your campaigns, tailor ads to specific audiences, and optimize your performance over time.

As you navigate the intricacies of the Google Ads platform, keep in mind that this chapter is just the beginning of your journey. In the following chapters, we'll delve into keyword research, crafting compelling ad copy, creating effective landing pages, and much more. With a solid understanding of the platform's fundamentals, you're well on your way to launching successful Google Ads campaigns that drive results.

Chapter 2: Setting Goals and Strategy

In this chapter, we'll dive deep into the strategic aspects of your Google Ads campaigns. Success begins with a clear vision and a well-defined plan. We'll guide you through the process of setting goals, understanding your target audience, and developing a comprehensive advertising strategy that aligns with your business objectives.

Defining Clear Advertising Goals

Before you launch any campaign, it's essential to define your goals. What do you want to achieve with your Google Ads efforts? Consider these common advertising goals:

1. **Increase Website Traffic:** Drive more visitors to your website to increase brand exposure and engagement.
2. **Generate Leads:** Collect user information for potential follow-up and conversions.
3. **Boost Sales:** Encourage immediate purchases through your online store.
4. **Raise Brand Awareness:** Introduce your brand to a broader audience and create recognition.
5. **Promote App Installs:** Drive downloads of your mobile app to expand your user base.
6. **Drive Store Visits:** Attract local customers to your physical store through online promotions.

By setting clear goals, you'll be better equipped to measure your campaign's success and tailor your strategies accordingly.

Identifying Target Audiences and Personas

Understanding your target audience is pivotal to crafting effective ad campaigns. Define your audience based on demographics, interests, behaviors, and buying intent. To further refine your targeting, create buyer personas—fictional representations of your ideal customers. Consider factors like age, gender, location, interests, challenges, and motivations.

For example, if you're a fitness apparel brand targeting young adults interested in staying fit, your buyer persona might be "Active Amy," a 25-year-old who loves outdoor activities and values eco-friendly products.

Developing a Comprehensive Advertising Strategy

With your goals and audience in mind, it's time to develop a holistic advertising strategy:

1. **Keyword Research:** Conduct thorough keyword research to identify the terms your target audience is searching for. Use tools like Google Keyword Planner to find relevant keywords with high search volumes.
2. **Competitive Analysis:** Study your competitors' strategies to identify gaps and opportunities. Analyze their keywords, ad copy, and landing pages.
3. **Budget Allocation:** Determine your budget for each campaign and allocate funds based on your goals. Consider factors like seasonality and campaign duration.
4. **Campaign Structure:** Organize your campaigns and ad groups logically. Keep ad groups focused on specific products or services to enhance relevance.
5. **Ad Copy and Creative:** Craft compelling ad copy that resonates with your audience's needs and emotions. Use persuasive language, highlight benefits, and include a clear call-to-action.
6. **Landing Pages:** Design landing pages that align with your ad's message and provide a seamless user experience. Ensure fast loading times and clear conversion paths.

7. **Ad Extensions:** Take advantage of ad extensions to provide additional information and increase click-through rates.
8. **Testing and Optimization:** Regularly monitor your campaign's performance and make data-driven adjustments. Test different ad variations, keywords, and landing page elements to find the winning combination.
9. **Tracking and Measurement:** Implement conversion tracking to measure the success of your campaigns. Use tools like Google Analytics to gain deeper insights into user behavior.
10. **Long-Term Strategy:** Plan for the long term by assessing your campaigns' performance over time and adjusting your strategy based on trends and changing business goals.

Remember, a well-crafted advertising strategy is dynamic and adaptable. As you gather data and insights, be ready to tweak your approach to ensure your campaigns are always aligned with your business's evolving needs.

In the next chapter, we'll delve into the critical process of keyword research and selection, where we'll explore how to identify the right keywords that will propel your campaigns to success. By combining a solid strategy with precise keyword targeting, you'll be well on your way to mastering Google Ads and achieving your business objectives.

Chapter 3: Keyword Research and Selection

In this chapter, we'll explore the foundation of any successful Google Ads campaign: keyword research. By understanding the significance of keyword research, utilizing effective tools, and evaluating competition and search volume, you'll be equipped to choose the right keywords that drive relevant traffic and conversions to your campaigns.

The Importance of Keyword Research

Keyword research is the cornerstone of your Google Ads campaigns. It involves identifying the specific words and phrases that users enter into search engines when looking for products, services, or information related to your business. Effective keyword research offers several key benefits:

1. **Relevance:** By targeting relevant keywords, you ensure that your ads are shown to users who are genuinely interested in what you offer.
2. **Visibility:** Properly chosen keywords help your ads appear in search results, increasing your brand's visibility and chances of attracting clicks.
3. **Cost Efficiency:** Focusing on the right keywords prevents you from wasting budget on irrelevant clicks and ensures a higher return on investment.
4. **User Intent:** Keyword research reveals user intent, allowing you to tailor your ad messaging to match what users are looking for.

Types of Keywords

In Google Ads, keywords are the words and phrases you choose to trigger your ads to show when users search on Google. There are several types of keywords you can use to target your ads effectively:

1. Broad Match:

- Example: running shoes
- Ads may show for variations, synonyms, related searches, and relevant searches even if they don't include the exact keyword.

2. Broad Match Modifier:

- Example: +running +shoes
- Ads will show for searches that include both (or more) of the modified terms in any order. This offers more control than broad match.

3. Phrase Match:

- Example: "running shoes"
- Ads will show for searches that include the keyword phrase in the exact order specified, but other words can be present before or after the phrase.

4. Exact Match:

- Example: [running shoes]
- Ads will show only for searches that match the keyword exactly, with no additional words before, after, or in between.

5. Negative Match:

- Example: -cheap
- Use negative keywords to prevent your ads from showing for certain search terms. For example, if you're selling premium products, you might use -cheap to exclude searches looking for cheaper alternatives.

6. Broad Match Negative:

- Example: -basketball
- This prevents your ad from showing if certain keywords are in the user's search, even if the rest of the search matches your targeting.

7. Phrase Match Negative:

- Example: -"running shoes"
- Prevents your ad from showing if the user's search contains the specified phrase.

8. Exact Match Negative:

- Example: -[used shoes]
- Prevents your ad from showing for searches that exactly match the negative keyword.

Using a mix of these keyword types allows you to control the reach and specificity of your ads. Broad match helps you capture a wider audience, while exact match provides precise targeting. Negative keywords help you filter out irrelevant searches. When building your keyword strategy, consider using a combination of these types to ensure your ads reach the right audience and drive valuable clicks and conversions.

Tools for Effective Keyword Discovery

Several tools can aid in your keyword research efforts:

1. **Google Keyword Planner:** This free tool helps you discover new keywords, assess their search volume, and estimate their performance.
2. **Keyword Research Tools:** Third-party tools like SEMrush, Ahrefs, and Moz offer comprehensive keyword insights, including competition data and related terms.
3. **Google Search Suggestions:** When you start typing in Google's search bar, it offers autocomplete suggestions based on popular queries, which can give you ideas for relevant keywords.
4. **Competitor Analysis:** Examine your competitors' websites and ads to identify keywords they're targeting.

5. **Customer Feedback and Surveys:** Listen to your existing customers and conduct surveys to identify the language they use when searching for products or services like yours.

Evaluating Keyword Competition and Search Volume

When choosing keywords, consider the balance between competition and search volume:

1. **Keyword Competition:** High competition indicates that many advertisers are bidding for the same keyword. While these keywords may yield substantial traffic, they can also be more costly. Low-competition keywords may be easier to rank for but could have lower search volumes.
2. **Search Volume:** This represents how often a keyword is searched for in a specific time frame. High search volume can bring more potential visitors, but it's essential to ensure the keywords align with your campaign goals.

To evaluate keywords effectively, consider long-tail keywords (more specific phrases) in addition to broad terms. Long-tail keywords often have lower competition and can yield highly targeted traffic.

Incorporate a mix of both high-volume and long-tail keywords to strike a balance between visibility and relevance. Keep in mind that keyword research is not a one-time task; regularly revisit and update your keyword list to adapt to changing trends and user behavior.

With a strong understanding of the significance of keyword research, the tools at your disposal, and the ability to assess competition and search volume, you're well-prepared to proceed to the next stages of crafting your Google Ads campaigns. In the upcoming chapter, we'll delve into the art of crafting compelling ad copy that captures your audience's attention and drives engagement.

Here are examples of different types of keywords that you might consider for your Google Ads campaigns in various industries:

1. **E-commerce - Clothing:**
   - High-Volume Keyword: "buy men's jeans"
   - Long-Tail Keyword: "slim fit black jeans for men"
   - Specific Model Keyword: "Levi's 501 jeans price"
2. **Local Services - Dentist:**
   - High-Volume Keyword: "dentist near me"
   - Long-Tail Keyword: "best pediatric dentist in [city]"
   - Service Keyword: "teeth whitening treatment cost"
3. **Online Courses - Photography:**
   - High-Volume Keyword: "online photography courses"
   - Long-Tail Keyword: "portrait photography tips for beginners"
   - Course Keyword: "digital photography masterclass"
4. **Travel - Vacation Rentals:**
   - High-Volume Keyword: "vacation rentals in [destination]"
   - Long-Tail Keyword: "beachfront cabin rentals in [location]"
   - Amenity Keyword: "pet-friendly vacation homes"
5. **Tech Gadgets - Smartphone Accessories:**
   - High-Volume Keyword: "best smartphone accessories"
   - Long-Tail Keyword: "wireless charging pads for iPhone 13"
   - Brand/Model Keyword: "Samsung Galaxy S21 case"
6. **Fitness - Home Workouts:**
   - High-Volume Keyword: "home workouts"
   - Long-Tail Keyword: "30-minute HIIT workouts at home"
   - Equipment Keyword: "resistance bands exercises for beginners"
7. **Food - Healthy Recipes:**
   - High-Volume Keyword: "healthy dinner recipes"
   - Long-Tail Keyword: "low-carb vegetarian recipes for weight loss"
   - Ingredient Keyword: "quinoa salad recipe with avocado"

Remember, the choice of keywords should align with your campaign goals and target audience. It's important to strike a balance between high-volume keywords that generate significant traffic and long-tail keywords that attract more specific, motivated users. Additionally, you can use negative keywords to exclude terms that are not relevant to your offering, ensuring your ads are shown to the right audience.

Chapter 4: Crafting Compelling Ad Copy

In this chapter, we'll delve into the art of creating ad copy that captivates your audience, draws them in, and persuades them to take action. Crafting compelling ad copy involves understanding the elements of a successful ad, writing attention-grabbing headlines, and crafting persuasive ad descriptions that resonate with your target audience.

Elements of a Successful Ad

A successful ad comprises several key elements that work together to communicate your message effectively and drive user engagement:

1. **Headline:** The first thing users see. It should be attention-grabbing and relevant to the user's search intent.
2. **Description:** The main body of text that expands on the headline and entices users to learn more or take action.
3. **URL Display:** The visible website link users see. It should reflect the landing page's content.
4. **Call-to-Action (CTA):** A clear instruction that prompts users to take a specific action, such as "Shop Now," "Sign Up," or "Learn More."

Writing Attention-Grabbing Headlines

Your headline is the initial hook that determines whether users click on your ad. Here are strategies for creating attention-grabbing headlines:

1. **Relevance:** Ensure your headline directly relates to the user's search query.

2. **Highlight Benefits:** Convey the value users will gain from your product or service.

3. **Include Keywords:** Incorporate relevant keywords to establish relevance and boost quality score.

4. **Urgency:** Use words like "limited time offer" or "last chance" to create a sense of urgency.

5. **Numbers and Stats:** Use numbers to quantify benefits, e.g., "Save 20% on All Items."

6. **Question or Solution:** Pose a question that resonates with users' pain points or offer a solution to their problem.

7. **Emotion and Storytelling:** Evoke emotions or tell a brief story to connect with users on a personal level.

Crafting Persuasive Ad Descriptions

The description complements your headline, providing more details and reasons for users to engage with your ad. Here's how to craft persuasive ad descriptions:

1. **Focus on Benefits:** Clearly communicate how users will benefit from your product or service.
2. **Unique Selling Proposition (USP):** Highlight what sets you apart from competitors.
3. **Conciseness:** Keep your description concise and to the point.
4. **Features and Value:** Mention specific features while emphasizing their value to the user.
5. **Call-to-Action:** Reinforce your CTA in the description to guide users toward the desired action.
6. **Social Proof:** If applicable, mention customer reviews, ratings, or endorsements.

7. **Dynamic Keyword Insertion:** Use this feature to insert the user's search query into the ad, making it more relevant.

By mastering the art of crafting compelling ad copy, you'll be able to create ads that resonate with your audience, increase click-through rates, and drive conversions. In the next chapter, we'll focus on creating high-quality landing pages that complement your ad copy and provide a seamless user experience, further enhancing the effectiveness of your Google Ads campaigns.

Here's a step-by-step guide to creating an ad copy in Google Ads:

Step 1: Sign in to Your Google Ads Account

Log in to your Google Ads account using your credentials.

Step 2: Navigate to Campaigns

Click on "Campaigns" in the left navigation menu to access your campaigns.

Step 3: Choose the Campaign

Select the campaign in which you want to create a new ad. If you haven't created a campaign yet, you can create one by clicking the "+ New Campaign" button.

Step 4: Navigate to Ads

Within the selected campaign, click on the "Ads & extensions" tab in the campaign menu.

Step 5: Click the "+ New Ad" Button

Click the "+ New Ad" button to create a new ad within the chosen campaign.

Step 6: Choose Ad Type

Select the type of ad you want to create. You can choose from options like Search ad, Display ad, Responsive search ad, and more. For this example, let's choose a Search ad.

Step 7: Enter Final URL

Enter the final URL that users will be directed to when they click on your ad. This should be a relevant landing page that matches your ad's content.

Step 8: Write Headline 1 and 2

Enter the headlines for your ad. Keep in mind that each headline has character limits. Craft headlines that are attention-grabbing and relevant to the user's search intent.

Step 9: Write Description

Write a compelling ad description that expands on your headlines and highlights the benefits of your product or service. Be concise and persuasive.

Step 10: Add Path Fields (if applicable)

Depending on the ad type, you might have the option to add path fields (often referred to as "path 1" and "path 2"). These are additional elements that can appear in your ad's URL, helping users understand where they'll be taken after clicking.

Step 11: Add Ad Extensions (optional but recommended)

Enhance your ad by adding extensions such as site link extensions, callout extensions, structured snippet extensions, and more. Extensions provide additional information and increase the visibility of your ad.

Step 12: Preview and Save

Preview your ad to ensure it looks as expected. Make any necessary adjustments. Once you're satisfied with the ad copy, click the "Save" button to save your ad.

Step 13: Review and Publish

Review your ad one final time before publishing. Ensure that all elements, including URLs and text, are accurate. If everything looks good, click the "Publish" or "Save and Continue" button to make your ad live.

Congratulations! You've successfully created an ad copy in Google Ads. Remember to continually monitor your ad's performance and make adjustments based on the data to optimize your campaigns for better results.

Here are examples of successful Google ad copies across different industries:

E-commerce - Clothing: Headline: "Upgrade Your Style with Trendy Summer Outfits" Description: "Shop our latest collection of summer fashion. Get 20% off your first order. Limited time offer!"

Local Services - Plumbing: Headline: "24/7 Emergency Plumbing Services" Description: "Experienced plumbers ready to solve your plumbing woes anytime. Call now for a free quote!"

Online Courses - Digital Marketing: Headline: "Boost Your Career with Digital Marketing Skills" Description: "Learn SEO, social media, and more. Enroll today for 50% off. Start your journey to success!"

Travel - Vacation Rentals: Headline: "Escape to Paradise - Vacation Rentals in [Destination]" Description: "Book your dream vacation rental today. Oceanfront properties with unbeatable views!"

Tech Gadgets - Smartphones: Headline: "Unleash Innovation with the New [Brand] Smartphone" Description: "Experience cutting-edge features, stunning camera, and lightning-fast performance. Order now!"

Fitness - Home Workouts: Headline: "Stay Fit at Home with Expert Guided Workouts" Description: "Get in shape with our virtual fitness classes. Join our community and achieve your goals!"

Food Delivery - Healthy Meals: Headline: "Delicious and Nutritious Meals Delivered to Your Doorstep" Description: "Healthy eating made easy. Fresh ingredients, chef-crafted meals. Order now for a healthier you!"

Financial Services - Personal Loans: Headline: "Get the Funds You Need, When You Need Them" Description: "Flexible personal loans for any situation. Low rates, fast approval. Apply online today!"

Remember, successful ad copies are tailored to the audience, offer value, and include a clear call-to-action. The examples above use attention-grabbing headlines, highlight benefits, and create a sense of urgency or exclusivity. However, what works best can vary based on your industry, target audience, and campaign goals. Use these examples as inspiration and adapt them to your unique business and offerings.

Chapter 5: Creating High-Quality Landing Pages

In this chapter, we'll explore the critical aspect of creating landing pages that not only captivate your audience but also drive conversions. You'll learn about designing landing pages that convert, aligning them with your ad copy, and implementing effective call-to-actions (CTAs) to guide users toward the desired action.

Designing Landing Pages that Convert

A landing page serves as the bridge between your ad and the user's desired action. To design landing pages that convert effectively:

1. **Simplicity:** Keep the design clean and clutter-free, focusing on the core message and call-to-action.
2. **Relevance:** Ensure the landing page content aligns with the ad that brought users to it. Match headlines, keywords, and visuals.
3. **Clear Hierarchy:** Use a clear hierarchy of information, guiding users' attention toward key elements like headlines and CTAs.
4. **Visuals:** Incorporate relevant images or videos that enhance understanding and appeal to emotions.
5. **Trust Indicators:** Include trust elements such as customer reviews, ratings, awards, and security certifications.
6. **Mobile Optimization:** Ensure your landing page is responsive and optimized for mobile devices, as many users access the internet through their phones.

Aligning Landing Pages with Ad Copy

A seamless transition from ad to landing page enhances user experience and conversion rates:

1. **Consistent Messaging:** Use the same language, tone, and visuals from your ad copy on the landing page.
2. **Keyword Alignment:** If a user clicked on an ad due to a specific keyword, ensure that keyword is present on the landing page.
3. **Benefits:** Highlight the benefits users were promised in the ad to reinforce their decision.
4. **Offer Continuity:** If you're promoting an offer, ensure it's prominently displayed on the landing page.

Implementing Effective Call-to-Actions (CTAs)

CTAs are crucial for guiding users to take action. Here's how to create effective CTAs:

1. **Clarity:** Make your CTA clear and concise, leaving no room for confusion.
2. **Action-Oriented Language:** Use action verbs that prompt users to take immediate action.
3. **Placement:** Position the CTA prominently on the page, preferably above the fold.
4. **Contrast:** Use contrasting colors to make the CTA stand out from the rest of the page.
5. **Urgency:** Create a sense of urgency or scarcity in the CTA, encouraging users to act quickly.
6. **Value Proposition:** Communicate the value users will gain by clicking the CTA.
7. **Minimal Fields:** If you're using a form, keep it concise with only essential fields to reduce friction.

By crafting landing pages that align with your ad copy and incorporate effective CTAs, you'll create a seamless user journey that maximizes conversions. In the next chapter, we'll delve into the world of bidding strategies and budget allocation, providing you with insights to optimize your campaign's performance and achieve your desired results.

Chapter 6: Understanding Ad Campaign Types

In this chapter, we'll explore various ad campaign types available within Google Ads. Each campaign type has its unique purpose and benefits, allowing you to tailor your advertising efforts to different goals. We'll dive into Search Ads, Display Ads, Video Ads, Shopping Ads, and App Promotion Ads, helping you understand when and how to use each type effectively.

Search Ads: Reaching Users at the Right Moment

Search ads appear in Google's search results when users enter relevant search queries. They are text-based and highly targeted:

- **Benefits:** Reach users actively searching for products or information. Show your ads when they're most likely to convert.
- **Strategy:** Utilize relevant keywords, write compelling ad copy, and include a strong call-to-action.

Display Ads: Building Brand Awareness

Display ads appear on websites, apps, and YouTube videos within Google's Display Network. They incorporate images, videos, and interactive elements:

- **Benefits:** Build brand awareness, reach a wider audience, and showcase visual content.
- **Strategy:** Design visually appealing ads, use engaging visuals, and target specific demographics or interests.

Video Ads: Engaging Through Visual Storytelling

Video ads appear on YouTube and across Google's network. They are a powerful way to engage users through visual storytelling:

- **Benefits:** Convey complex messages, capture attention, and evoke emotions through visuals and sound.
- **Strategy:** Create compelling videos that resonate with your audience. Choose different video ad formats based on your goals.

Shopping Ads: Showcasing Products Effectively

Shopping ads showcase products and their prices directly within Google's search results:

- **Benefits:** Display product images, prices, and information, making it easy for users to compare and choose.
- **Strategy:** Set up a Google Merchant Center account, create product feeds, and optimize your product data.

App Promotion Ads: Driving App Installs and Engagement

App promotion ads encourage users to download and engage with your mobile app:

- **Benefits:** Drive app installs, engagement, and conversions among mobile users.

- **Strategy:** Use compelling ad copy, showcase app features, and target relevant audiences.

Each campaign type caters to specific goals and audience segments. By understanding the strengths of each type, you can create a well-rounded advertising strategy that reaches users at various touchpoints and stages of their journey. In the next chapter, we'll explore the intricacies of budget allocation and bidding strategies, helping you make the most of your advertising budget and optimize your campaigns for maximum results.

Chapter 7

Mastering Ad Extensions

In this chapter, we'll delve into the world of ad extensions, powerful tools that enhance your ads by providing additional information and opportunities for engagement. We'll cover various types of ad extensions, including Sitelink, Callout, Structured Snippet, Location, Affiliate, and Promotion Extensions. By mastering these extensions, you can make your ads more informative, attractive, and actionable.

Using Sitelink, Callout, and Structured Snippet Extensions

1. **Sitelink Extensions:**
   o These additional links direct users to specific pages on your website.
   o Benefits: Offer users multiple options to explore different sections of your site.
   o Strategy: Choose relevant landing pages, use clear and concise text, and align with user intent.

2. **Callout Extensions:**
   o Callouts highlight key information about your products, services, or offerings.
   o Benefits: Showcase unique selling points, promotions, or free shipping offers.
   o Strategy: Emphasize benefits, keep text short, and create urgency if applicable.

3. **Structured Snippet Extensions:**

- These snippets provide more context about specific aspects of your offerings.

- Benefits: Give users a quick overview of categories, features, or services.

- Strategy: Use appropriate headers and descriptions to highlight different offerings.

Leveraging Location and Affiliate Extensions

1. **Location Extensions:**
   - Display your business's physical locations alongside your ad.
   - Benefits: Drive offline visits by providing location details directly in the ad.
   - Strategy: Set up Google My Business and link it to your ads for accurate location information.
2. **Affiliate Location Extensions:**
   - Highlight nearby retailers that sell your products.
   - Benefits: Help users find your products in local stores.
   - Strategy: Collaborate with affiliates and ensure accurate location data.

Showcasing Additional Information with Promotion Extensions

1. **Promotion Extensions:**
   - Display specific promotions or offers within your ads.
   - Benefits: Capture users' attention with limited-time deals or discounts.
   - Strategy: Use clear and compelling promotions, include details, and set start and end dates.

By utilizing these various ad extensions, you can enrich your ads with additional details, make them more relevant, and provide users with more reasons to click. Ad extensions not only improve the visibility and performance of your ads but also enhance the user experience, driving more engagement and conversions. In the upcoming chapter, we'll delve into the importance of tracking and measuring your campaigns, helping you understand how to analyze data and optimize your strategies for even better results.

Sitelink Extensions:

- "Shop Women's Clothing"
- "Explore Summer Collection"
- "View Latest Arrivals"
- "Browse Men's Footwear"

Callout Extensions:

- "Free Shipping on Orders Over $50"
- "24/7 Customer Support"
- "Price Match Guarantee"
- "Easy Returns & Exchanges"

Structured Snippet Extensions:

- "Product Categories: Dresses, Shoes, Accessories"
- "Service Types: Web Design, SEO, Social Media"
- "Cuisine Types: Italian, Asian, Mexican"
- "Room Types: Deluxe Suite, Standard Room, Family Suite"

Location Extensions:

- "Visit Us: 123 Main Street"
- "Find Our Store: [Store Name]"
- "Explore Our Showroom: [City] Location"
- "Shop In-Person at [Location Name]"

Affiliate Location Extensions:

- "Available at [Retailer Name] Stores Near You"
- "Buy Our Products at [Affiliate Retailer]"
- "Find [Brand] Products at [Retailer] Locations"
- "Shop [Brand] Products at [Retailer] Outlets"

Promotion Extensions:

- "Limited Time Offer: 20% Off Sitewide!"
- "Get 50% Off on Select Styles"
- "Summer Sale: Save Big on Swimwear"
- "Back-to-School Discount: 15% Off Backpacks"

These examples showcase how each type of ad extension can be used to provide users with more information, incentives, and options to engage with your ads. Customize the content of your extensions to align with your business goals and the specific offerings you want to promote.

Chapter 8

Bidding Strategies and Budgeting

In this chapter, we'll delve into the crucial aspects of bidding strategies and budget allocation within your Google Ads campaigns. We'll explore the differences between manual and automated bidding strategies, discuss how to set realistic budgets for your campaigns, and provide insights into adjusting bids for optimal performance.

Manual vs. Automated Bidding Strategies

1. **Manual Bidding:**
   o   With manual bidding, you set the bids for your keywords and ad groups based on your understanding of your target audience, competition, and campaign goals.
   o   Benefits: Full control over bids, ideal for experienced advertisers who prefer a hands-on approach.
   o   Strategy: Regularly monitor and adjust bids based on performance data and market trends.
2. **Automated Bidding:**
   o   Automated bidding uses machine learning to adjust bids automatically based on real-time data.
   o   Benefits: Saves time, optimizes bids for conversions or clicks, and adapts to changing conditions.
   o   Strategy: Choose the appropriate automated bidding strategy (e.g., Target CPA, Target ROAS) based on your goals.

Setting Realistic Budgets for Campaigns

1. **Consider Business Goals:** Align your budget with your campaign objectives, whether it's driving sales, leads, or brand awareness.
2. **Analyze Historical Data:** Review past campaign performance to determine what has worked and allocate budgets accordingly.
3. **Keyword Research:** Estimate costs per click and potential clicks to gauge budget requirements.

4. **Test and Adjust:** Start with a manageable budget, test different strategies, and gradually allocate more budget to high-performing campaigns.

Adjusting Bids for Optimal Performance

1. **Monitor Performance:** Regularly review your campaigns' performance metrics, such as click-through rates, conversion rates, and return on ad spend (ROAS).
2. **Bid Adjustment Factors:**
   o Device: Adjust bids based on how different devices contribute to conversions.
   o Location: Modify bids for locations with higher or lower conversion rates.
   o Time of Day/Week: Increase bids during peak hours or days for better visibility.
3. **Use Bid Modifiers:** Utilize bid modifiers within automated bidding strategies to prioritize certain segments.
4. **Competitor Analysis:** Monitor competitive bids and adjust your bids to remain competitive.
5. **Experiment and Optimize:** Test bid adjustments and analyze the impact on performance before making significant changes.

Remember, finding the right bidding strategy and budget requires ongoing testing and optimization. Be prepared to adjust your approach based on data insights and market dynamics. In the next chapter, we'll dive into the world of ad performance tracking and data analysis, empowering you to make informed decisions and continually improve the effectiveness of your Google Ads campaigns.

Here are budgeting examples based on different scenarios and data insights:

Scenario 1: E-commerce Campaign with Historical Data

Suppose you're running an e-commerce campaign and have historical data to work with:

- **Average Conversion Rate:** 4%
- **Average Cost Per Click (CPC):** $1.50
- **Desired Conversions per Day:** 20

Budget Calculation: Daily Budget = (Desired Conversions / Conversion Rate) * CPC Daily Budget = (20 / 0.04) * $1.50 = $750

In this scenario, setting a daily budget of $750 should help you achieve your goal of 20 conversions per day based on historical data.

Scenario 2: New Campaign with Limited Budget

If you're launching a new campaign with a limited budget, consider a conservative approach:

- **Average Cost Per Click (CPC):** $2.00
- **Daily Budget:** $30

Since it's a new campaign, start with a limited budget to test the waters and gather data. Monitor the performance and adjust the budget based on the campaign's initial results.

Scenario 3: Competitive Market with High CPC

In a competitive market, you might need a larger budget to stay competitive:

- **Average Cost Per Click (CPC):** $5.00
- **Desired Clicks per Day:** 100

Budget Calculation: Daily Budget = Desired Clicks * CPC Daily Budget = 100 * $5.00 = $500

In this scenario, allocating a daily budget of $500 would help you secure around 100 clicks per day in a competitive market with higher CPC.

Scenario 4: Seasonal Campaign with Variable Demand

For a seasonal campaign, adjust your budget based on demand fluctuations:

- **Average Conversion Rate:** 3%
- **Average Cost Per Click (CPC):** $1.75
- **Desired Conversions per Day:** 10 (Off-season) / 30 (Peak season)

Budget Calculation (Off-season): Daily Budget = (Desired Conversions / Conversion Rate) * CPC Daily Budget = (10 / 0.03) * $1.75 = $583.33

Budget Calculation (Peak season): Daily Budget = (Desired Conversions / Conversion Rate) * CPC Daily Budget = (30 / 0.03) * $1.75 = $1,750

Adjust your budget based on the season to ensure you're allocating more resources during peak demand periods.

These examples showcase how budgeting can be tailored to different scenarios and data insights. Remember, budget allocation is a dynamic process, and it's essential to continuously monitor and adjust based on performance data and market trends.

Chapter 9

Monitoring and Optimization

In this chapter, we'll dive deep into the critical process of monitoring and optimizing your Google Ads campaigns. You'll learn how to effectively track conversions and key performance indicators (KPIs), analyze performance data, and utilize A/B testing to optimize your ads for better results.

Tracking Conversions and KPIs

1. **Define Conversions:** Clearly define what actions you consider as conversions, whether they're sales, sign-ups, downloads, or other valuable interactions.

2. **Set Up Conversion Tracking:** Use Google Ads' conversion tracking tools to monitor the actions users take after clicking your ads.

3. **Choose KPIs:** Determine key performance indicators (KPIs) that align with your campaign goals, such as click-through rates (CTR), conversion rates, cost per conversion, and return on ad spend (ROAS).

Analyzing Performance Data

1. **Campaign-Level Analysis:** Review overall campaign metrics, budget utilization, and performance trends.
2. **Ad Group Analysis:** Analyze ad group performance to identify which groups are driving conversions and which might need adjustments.
3. **Keyword Analysis:** Evaluate keyword performance by assessing click-through rates, conversion rates, and cost-effectiveness.
4. **Device and Location Insights:** Understand how different devices and locations impact your campaign's performance.

A/B Testing: Optimizing Ads for Better Results

1. **Ad Copy Testing:** Create multiple variations of your ad copy to test different headlines, descriptions, and CTAs.
2. **Landing Page Testing:** Test different landing pages to determine which ones result in higher conversions.
3. **Ad Extension Testing:** Experiment with different ad extensions to see which ones contribute to improved performance.
4. **Bidding Strategy Testing:** Try different bidding strategies to assess which one aligns best with your goals.

Optimization Strategies

1. **Budget Reallocation:** Allocate more budget to high-performing campaigns and adjust or pause underperforming ones.
2. **Keyword Optimization:** Regularly update and refine your keyword list based on performance data.
3. **Negative Keywords:** Continuously add negative keywords to exclude irrelevant searches and improve targeting.
4. **Ad Schedule Adjustments:** Modify ad schedules to focus on peak times of user activity.
5. **Bid Adjustments:** Adjust bids based on device, location, and time of day to optimize for conversions.
6. **Quality Score Improvement:** Optimize your landing pages and ad relevance to improve Quality Scores and lower costs.

Optimizing your Google Ads campaigns is crucial for achieving better results and maximizing your return on investment.

Here are some of the best ways to optimize your campaigns effectively:

1. Regular Monitoring:

Keep a close eye on your campaign performance, checking key metrics like CTR, conversion rates, and cost per conversion.

2. Refine Keyword Strategy:

Regularly review your keyword performance and refine your keyword list. Pause low-performing keywords and focus on those generating conversions.

3. Quality Ad Copy:

Continuously test different ad copy variations to identify what resonates best with your audience. Use compelling headlines and persuasive descriptions.

4. Landing Page Optimization:

Ensure your landing pages are relevant to your ad copy and provide a seamless user experience. Test different landing page layouts and content.

5. Utilize Ad Extensions:

Take advantage of various ad extensions to provide more information and enhance your ads' visibility and click-through rates.

6. Mobile Optimization:

Given the increasing mobile usage, ensure your campaigns are optimized for mobile devices with responsive designs and mobile-specific ad copy.

7. A/B Testing:

Experiment with different ad elements, such as headlines, images, CTAs, and landing pages. A/B testing helps identify what works best.

8. Negative Keywords:

Regularly update your list of negative keywords to filter out irrelevant searches and improve targeting.

9. Bid Adjustments:

Use bid adjustments for devices, locations, and ad schedules to optimize bids based on performance trends.

10. Ad Schedule Optimization:

Analyze when your ads perform best and adjust ad schedules to focus on peak activity times.

11. Review Search Terms:

Regularly review the search terms that trigger your ads. Add relevant terms as keywords and exclude irrelevant ones with negative keywords.

12. Competitor Analysis:

Monitor your competitors' ads and strategies to stay competitive and adapt to changes in the market.

13. Conversion Tracking:

Set up and track conversions accurately to measure the effectiveness of your campaigns and make data-driven decisions.

14. Budget Reallocation:

Allocate budget to well-performing campaigns while scaling back on underperforming ones.

15. Test Bidding Strategies:

Experiment with different bidding strategies based on your campaign goals, such as Target CPA or Target ROAS.

16. Geographic Targeting:

Adjust bids and ad content based on the performance of different geographic locations.

17. Ad Position:

Test different ad positions to find the balance between visibility and cost-effectiveness.

18. Monitor Competitor Activity:

Keep an eye on your competitors' ad placements and strategies to stay ahead in the game.

Remember that optimization is an ongoing process. Regularly analyze data, test new strategies, and adapt to changes in the market to continually improve the performance of your Google Ads campaigns.

Chapter 10

Advanced Techniques and Tips

In this final chapter, we'll explore advanced techniques and tips to take your Google Ads campaigns to the next level. These strategies will help you leverage the full potential of Google Ads to reach your target audience effectively and drive better results.

Remarketing: Reconnecting with Interested Users

1. **Dynamic Remarketing:** Show personalized ads to users who visited your site, featuring the specific products or services they viewed.
2. **Remarketing Lists for Search Ads (RLSA):** Adjust bids and ad copy for users who have previously interacted with your website.

Dynamic Search Ads: Targeting Relevant Searches Automatically

1. **Automatic Keyword Insertion:** Dynamically insert keywords from users' search queries into your ad copy for increased relevance.
2. **Automated Targeting:** Let Google's algorithm automatically match your ads to relevant search queries and landing pages.

Ad Schedule and Geo-Targeting: Reaching the Right Audience at the Right Time

1. **Ad Scheduling:** Adjust ad schedules to show ads during times when your target audience is most active.
2. **Geographic Targeting:** Target specific geographic areas where your potential customers are located.

Using Negative Keywords to Refine Audience Targeting

1. **Broad Match Modifier:** Use "+keyword" to ensure your ads show for variations of your keywords while excluding irrelevant terms.

2. **Regular Negative Keywords:** Continuously update your list of negative keywords to prevent your ads from showing for irrelevant searches.

Custom Audience Targeting: Tailoring Ads to Specific Segments

1. **Customer Match:** Upload a list of customer emails to target existing customers with tailored ads.
2. **Similar Audiences:** Reach new users who share similar characteristics with your existing customers.

Experiment with Ad Formats: Maximize Engagement

1. **Responsive Search Ads:** Create multiple headlines and descriptions to allow Google to test different combinations and show the most effective ads.
2. **Ad Variations:** Experiment with different ad formats and variations to determine what resonates best with your audience.

Utilize Ad Customizers: Enhancing Personalization

1. **Countdown Timers:** Create a sense of urgency by adding countdown timers to your ads for limited-time offers.
2. **Keyword Insertion:** Customize ads to include users' search keywords, making them more relevant and attention-grabbing.

By incorporating these advanced techniques and tips into your Google Ads strategy, you can refine your targeting, increase engagement, and ultimately achieve better results. Keep in mind that staying updated with the latest trends and features within the Google Ads platform will further empower you to stay ahead of the competition and continue driving success.

Chapter 11

Staying Up-to-Date with Google Ads

In this final chapter, we'll emphasize the importance of staying informed about Google Ads updates and continuously learning to adapt your strategies.

The world of digital advertising is dynamic, and keeping up-to-date with changes is crucial for maintaining successful campaigns.

Keeping Abreast of Google Ads Updates

1. **Official Google Resources:** Regularly check the official Google Ads blog, Help Center, and release notes to stay informed about new features, updates, and best practices.

2. **Google Ads Academy:** Explore the Google Ads Academy for free courses and certifications that cover various aspects of Google Ads, from basics to advanced strategies.

3. **Industry News and Forums:** Follow digital marketing blogs, forums, and industry news sources to stay informed about trends, updates, and insights.

Continuously Learning and Adapting Strategies

1. **Attend Webinars and Events:** Participate in webinars and industry events to learn from experts, gain insights, and connect with other advertisers.

2. **Experiment and Test:** Continuously test new strategies, ad formats, and targeting options to discover what works best for your specific business goals.

3. **Analyze and Optimize:** Regularly review campaign data, analyze performance metrics, and optimize based on insights to improve your results.

4. **Adapt to Changes:** As Google updates its algorithms and policies, be prepared to adapt your strategies to maintain compliance and effectiveness.

5. **Networking:** Engage with other digital marketers, join online communities, and participate in discussions to exchange knowledge and experiences.

6. **Feedback from Users:** Pay attention to feedback from users who engage with your ads. Adjust your strategies based on their responses and preferences.

Remember that the digital landscape is ever-evolving, and what works today may not work as effectively tomorrow.

By staying proactive and continuously learning, you'll be better equipped to navigate changes, seize opportunities, and maintain successful Google Ads campaigns that drive meaningful results for your business.

Chapter 12

Troubleshooting and Problem Solving

In this final chapter, we'll address common challenges that can arise in Google Ads campaigns and provide strategies for troubleshooting and solving ad performance issues. Overcoming these challenges is essential for maintaining the effectiveness of your campaigns.

Common Google Ads Challenges

1. **Low Click-Through Rate (CTR):** Your ads aren't generating enough clicks despite impressions.

2. **High Cost Per Click (CPC):** Your bids are resulting in higher costs for each click, affecting your budget.

3. **Low Conversion Rate:** While you're getting clicks, your ads aren't leading to desired actions.

4. **Ad Fatigue:** Your ads become less effective over time as users become accustomed to seeing them.

5. **Irrelevant Traffic:** Your ads are attracting users who aren't genuinely interested in your offerings.

6. **Low Quality Score:** Google rates your ads as less relevant, impacting your ad position and costs.

Strategies for Addressing Ad Performance Issues

1. **Review Ad Relevance:** Ensure your ad copy, keywords, and landing pages align with each other and deliver on user expectations.
2. **Keyword Optimization:** Regularly review and refine your keyword list to target the most relevant terms.
3. **Ad Copy Refresh:** Update your ad copy to keep it relevant and engaging for your target audience.
4. **Landing Page Optimization:** Improve landing page design, content, and user experience to boost conversion rates.
5. **Negative Keywords:** Use negative keywords to filter out irrelevant searches that are draining your budget.
6. **Experiment with Ad Formats:** Test different ad formats and variations to discover what resonates best with your audience.
7. **Bid Optimization:** Adjust bids based on performance data and bidding strategies to achieve better results.
8. **A/B Testing:** Continuously test different ad elements to identify what performs best and iterate accordingly.
9. **Ad Schedule Adjustment:** Modify ad schedules to focus on peak activity times and adjust bid adjustments accordingly.
10. **Competitor Analysis:** Monitor competitors' ads and strategies to identify opportunities for improvement.
11. **Quality Score Improvement:** Enhance ad relevance, landing page experience, and CTR to improve Quality Scores.
12. **Conversion Tracking Accuracy:** Ensure your conversion tracking is set up correctly to accurately measure campaign performance.

By identifying the challenges affecting your campaigns and implementing strategic solutions, you'll be better equipped to address performance issues and optimize your Google Ads campaigns for success. Regular monitoring, testing, and adaptation are key to maintaining a strong and effective online advertising presence.

Chapter 13: Scaling and Expanding Campaigns

In this chapter, we'll delve into strategies for scaling and expanding your successful Google Ads campaigns. As your campaigns prove effective, it's important to capitalize on their momentum and gradually broaden your reach to maximize your advertising impact.

Strategies for Scaling Successful Campaigns

1. **Budget Increment:** Gradually increase your campaign budgets to accommodate higher traffic and conversions as you scale.
2. **Expand Target Audience:** Identify additional segments within your target audience and tailor ad copy and targeting to resonate with them.
3. **Geographic Expansion:** Expand your geographic targeting to reach new regions or countries that align with your business goals.
4. **Keyword Expansion:** Introduce new, relevant keywords to capture additional search queries and expand your reach.
5. **Device and Platform Diversity:** Optimize your campaigns for various devices (desktop, mobile, tablet) and consider advertising on different platforms such as YouTube or the Display Network.

Introducing New Keywords and Ad Groups

1. **Long-Tail Keywords:** Incorporate more specific and niche keywords to capture users who are further along in the buying cycle.
2. **Seasonal Keywords:** Introduce keywords related to seasonal trends or holidays to tap into increased demand.
3. **Related Keywords:** Identify related terms and expand your keyword list to cover a broader spectrum of user queries.

Expanding to Different Ad Formats and Networks

1. **Display Network:** Extend your campaigns to the Google Display Network to reach users through image and text ads on various websites and apps.
2. **Video Ads:** Utilize video ads on YouTube to engage users through visual storytelling and tap into the platform's massive audience.
3. **Shopping Campaigns:** If you're an e-commerce business, consider setting up shopping campaigns to showcase products with images, prices, and descriptions.
4. **App Promotion Ads:** If you have a mobile app, expand your campaigns to promote app downloads and engagement.

Testing and Iteration

1. **Incremental Expansion:** Gradually introduce changes and new elements to monitor their impact and ensure you're maintaining positive results.
2. **Performance Analysis:** Continuously monitor new additions and evaluate their performance to identify what's working and what needs adjustment.
3. **Experimentation:** Test new strategies and formats on a smaller scale before implementing them across all your campaigns.

By carefully planning your expansion, testing new elements, and analyzing performance data, you can confidently scale your successful campaigns while maintaining control over their effectiveness. Remember that expansion should be a strategic process to ensure you're reaching new audiences and optimizing for the best possible outcomes.

Conclusion

In this comprehensive guide, we've embarked on a journey through the world of Google Ads, from understanding its power to crafting compelling ad copy, optimizing campaigns, and exploring advanced strategies. Let's recap the key takeaways and set the stage for your future success with Google Ads.

Recap of Key Takeaways

1. **Understanding Google Ads:** Google Ads is a powerful platform that allows you to reach your target audience with relevant ads when they're searching for products or services like yours.
2. **Setting Clear Goals:** Define specific and measurable goals for your campaigns to guide your strategies and measure success.
3. **Keyword Research:** Thoroughly research and select relevant keywords to target users who are actively searching for what you offer.
4. **Compelling Ad Copy:** Craft attention-grabbing headlines and persuasive ad descriptions that speak to your audience's needs and desires.
5. **Quality Landing Pages:** Design landing pages that align with your ad copy, deliver a seamless user experience, and drive conversions.
6. **Optimization Strategies:** Continuously monitor and analyze campaign performance, test different strategies, and optimize based on data insights.
7. **Advanced Techniques:** Explore advanced techniques such as remarketing, dynamic search ads, and ad extensions to enhance your campaigns.
8. **Scaling and Expansion:** Gradually scale successful campaigns by expanding to new keywords, ad formats, and networks while maintaining strategic control.
9. **Learning and Adaptation:** Stay up-to-date with Google Ads updates, continuously learn from industry resources, and adapt your strategies to changes.

Embracing a Future of Advertising Success with Google Ads

As you move forward, remember that success in Google Ads requires a combination of creativity, data analysis, and a willingness to adapt. Stay curious, experiment with different approaches, and don't hesitate to test new strategies. The digital landscape is ever-evolving, and your commitment to learning and improvement will be your greatest asset.

By harnessing the full potential of Google Ads, you're well on your way to reaching your business objectives, connecting with your target audience, and driving meaningful results. Embrace the future of advertising success with Google Ads, and keep building and refining your campaigns to achieve your goals. Your journey doesn't end here – it's just the beginning of a dynamic and rewarding partnership with Google Ads.

Appendix

In this appendix, you'll find valuable resources to enhance your understanding of Google Ads and continue your journey towards mastering successful advertising campaigns.

Glossary of Google Ads Terms

- **Impressions:** The number of times your ads are displayed to users.

- **Click-Through Rate (CTR):** The ratio of clicks to impressions, indicating the percentage of users who clicked on your ad after seeing it.

- **Conversion Rate:** The percentage of users who complete a desired action (e.g., purchase, sign-up) after clicking your ad.

- **Quality Score:** Google's rating of your ad's relevance and quality, impacting ad position and costs.

- **Keyword:** The words or phrases that trigger your ads to show when users search on Google.

- **Ad Group:** A collection of related keywords and ads within a campaign.

- **Campaign:** A set of ad groups sharing a common goal, budget, and targeting settings.

- **Ad Extensions:** Additional information like links, phone numbers, and promotions that can be added to your ads.

- **Remarketing:** Showing ads to users who previously interacted with your website.

- **Dynamic Search Ads:** Automatically generated ads based on the content of your website.

- **Conversion Tracking:** Tracking user actions that are valuable to your business, such as purchases or sign-ups.

Recommended Tools and Resources

- **Google Ads Help Center:** The official resource for learning about Google Ads features, settings, and troubleshooting.
- **Google Ads Academy:** Offers free courses and certifications covering various aspects of Google Ads.
- **Google Keyword Planner:** Helps you find relevant keywords and estimate their search volume.
- **Google Analytics:** Provides detailed insights into website traffic and user behavior.
- **Google Trends:** Shows search interest over time for specific terms.
- **SEMrush:** A comprehensive SEO and digital marketing tool that can assist with keyword research and competitive analysis.

Additional Reading for Continuous Learning

- **"Ultimate Guide to Google Ads" by Perry Marshall, Mike Rhodes, and Bryan Todd:** A comprehensive book covering everything from beginner to advanced Google Ads strategies.

- **"Advanced Google AdWords" by Brad Geddes:** A resource for in-depth strategies and tactics to maximize the impact of your Google Ads campaigns.
- **Industry Blogs and Websites:** Stay updated with blogs like Moz, Search Engine Journal, and PPC Hero for insights, news, and expert opinions on digital advertising.

Continuous learning and adaptation are essential in the ever-evolving field of digital advertising. Use these resources to deepen your knowledge, refine your strategies, and stay ahead of the curve in your journey to Google Ads success.

Here's a checklist to help you achieve success with Google Ads:

- **Campaign Planning:**
  - Define clear advertising goals.
  - Identify your target audience and buyer personas.
  - Research competitors and industry trends.
  - Set an appropriate campaign budget.
- **Keyword Research and Selection:**
  - Conduct thorough keyword research.
  - Choose a mix of broad, phrase, and exact match keywords.
  - Use negative keywords to filter out irrelevant searches.
- **Compelling Ad Copy:**
  - Write attention-grabbing headlines.
  - Craft persuasive ad descriptions.
  - Include a clear call-to-action (CTA).
  - Ensure ad copy aligns with landing page content.
- **Quality Landing Pages:**
  - Design landing pages for conversions.
  - Match landing page content to ad copy.
  - Implement clear and relevant CTAs.
- **Ad Extensions:**
  - Utilize sitelink, callout, and structured snippet extensions.
  - Include location and affiliate extensions if applicable.
  - Showcase promotions using promotion extensions.

- **Bidding Strategies and Budgeting:**
  - o Choose manual or automated bidding based on goals.
  - o Set realistic budgets for campaigns.
  - o Adjust bids for optimal performance.
- **Monitoring and Optimization:**
  - o Track conversions and key performance indicators (KPIs).
  - o Analyze performance data regularly.
  - o Conduct A/B testing for ads and landing pages.
  - o Optimize campaigns based on data insights.
- **Advanced Techniques and Tips:**
  - o Explore remarketing and dynamic search ads.
  - o Experiment with ad formats like video and display.
  - o Use negative keywords to refine targeting.
- **Scaling and Expansion:**
  - o Gradually increase campaign budgets for successful campaigns.
  - o Expand keyword list and target audience strategically.
  - o Introduce new ad formats and networks.
- **Staying Up-to-Date:**
  - o Stay informed about Google Ads updates.
  - o Continuously learn and adapt strategies.
  - o Attend webinars and industry events.
- **Troubleshooting and Problem Solving:**
  - o Address low CTR, high CPC, and low conversion rate.
  - o Analyze ad performance and optimize as needed.
- **Case Studies and Continuous Learning:**
  - o Study successful case studies for insights.
  - o Explore additional resources for learning.

By following this checklist, you'll have a comprehensive guide to help you navigate the world of Google Ads and work towards achieving successful and effective advertising campaigns.

Here are examples of ad copies based on data-driven strategies:

1. Keyword-Targeted Ad:

- Keyword: "Affordable Running Shoes"
- Headline: "Shop Affordable Running Shoes"
- Description: "Get top-quality running shoes at unbeatable prices. Limited-time offer! Browse our collection now."

2. Seasonal Ad with Keyword Insertion:

- Keyword: "Winter Jacket Deals"
- Headline: "Stay Warm with Winter Jacket Deals"
- Description: "Stay cozy this winter with our {=Winter Jacket} deals. Shop now and enjoy free shipping!"

3. Dynamic Remarketing Ad:

- Product Viewed: "Blue Sneakers"
- Headline: "Back for More? Check Out Our Blue Sneakers!"
- Description: "Your style, your choice! Explore our collection of {=Blue Sneakers}. Don't miss out!"

4. Limited-Time Promotion Ad:

- Product: "Smartphones"
- Headline: "Upgrade Your Tech: Save 20% on Smartphones!"
- Description: "Upgrade your device today and enjoy 20% off our latest smartphones. Offer ends soon."

5. Local Service Ad with Callout Extension:

- Service: "Plumbing Services"
- Headline: "Reliable Plumbing Services Near You"
- Description: "Need plumbing help? We offer fast and efficient {=Plumbing Services}. Call now for a free estimate."

6. App Promotion Ad with App Extension:

- App: "Meditation App"
- Headline: "Find Peace with Our Meditation App"
- Description: "Discover tranquility and mindfulness with our {=Meditation App}. Download now for a peaceful journey."

7. Location-Based Ad with Location Extension:

- Location: "New York Fitness Center"
- Headline: "Get Fit in NYC: Join Our Fitness Center"
- Description: "Achieve your fitness goals at {=New York Fitness Center}. Visit us today and enjoy a free trial."

8. Review-Driven Ad with Review Extension:

- Review: "5-Star Rated by Customers"
- Headline: "Experience Excellence: 5-Star Rated Products"
- Description: "Join our satisfied customers and choose {=5-Star Rated} products. Shop now for top quality."

These examples demonstrate how ad copy can be tailored to specific keywords, products, services, and promotions, utilizing techniques such as dynamic keyword insertion, location extensions, review extensions, and more. Remember that data-driven ad copy aims to align with user intent and capture their attention, ultimately leading to higher click-through rates and conversions.